Post-Dramatic Relationship Syndrome

Post-Dramatic Relationship Syndrome

How To Find Your Drama-Free Zone!

Valerie Maholmes PhD

2016 Valerie Maholmes PhD
Cover designed by Pixodign
ISBN: 0692775358
ISBN 13: 9780692775356
Library of Congress Control Number: 2016914642
Valerie Maholmes, Valerie Maholmes, MD

Dedication

To my sisters who dare to hope and love again and again.

Table of Contents

Preface

ONE DAY WHILE walking to the subway station, I ran into my friend Jillian. She's a sophisticated lady, always well dressed and looking totally in control. That day was an exception, as she unloaded this news—her long-term relationship with Jason had crumbled. "These men act like they don't have to meet their maker," she said. "Why would he take me through all of that if he knew he didn't want to be married? I was fine by myself; now I'm left with all these feelings to manage. I'll just have to find a way to get through this."

But before I could say a word or offer her a comforting hug, Jillian had put on her shades, tossed her hair back, straightened her shoulders, and, with an air of feigned determination, wistfully walked away.

Jillian's words and her wistful walking away inspired me to write *Post-Dramatic Relationship Syndrome: How to Find Your Drama-Free Zone*. I knew that Jillian's situation wasn't unique. Her story was a familiar one that countless other women of all ages and from all walks of life have experienced.

Drawing on my twenty-five years as a psychologist and educator and a lifetime of being a woman, I wanted to write a book that acknowledges these experiences and that provides insights for women to find their way back to wholeness and to be ready to love again. I often listened to women tell their stories of the situations that led to what I call dramatic relationships, and perhaps most importantly, what women *did* and how they *felt* after that relationship has ended. For the first time, there is a book that validates the challenges women experience after a relationship and gives it a name—Post-Dramatic Relationship Syndrome (PDRS)–that they can recognize, share, and embrace.

As you grapple with PDRS and search for a way forward, strength, and resolve, I want to be with you on your journey through these easy-to-read chapters. Each section of the book will take you through developmental stages of healing and empowerment: awareness, knowledge, resolution, and action. Also included are opportunities for personal reflection, analysis, and renewal to help you identify what you need and to track your progress. Reading this book will help you know that you're not alone in the way you feel and will provide useful strategies for getting over PDRS and getting on with life.

Acknowledgments

WRITING THIS BOOK was a labor of love many years in the making. I'd like to thank my friends and family for their support and encouragement. I'd especially like to thank my friend B. Denise Hawkins for her extraordinary editing skills and for her guidance and feedback. Above all, I wish to acknowledge all of my sisters and friends who had the courage to share their stories, inspiring me to write this book.

Did You Hear What Happened to Jillian?

DID YOU HEAR what happened to Jillian? Well, you know she and Jason had been an item for several years. I'm not sure what happened, but Jason is gone! Yes, that's right. He left her. No, he didn't storm out on her; he just eased away with no explanation at all. Jillian thought their relationship meant as much to Jason as it did to her. She was wrong. The sad part about it is that Jillian was happy being single and was not really concerned about getting married—she's really independent. Then she met Jason. He wooed her, wined and dined her, and swept her off her feet. Jillian started to think that maybe he was "the one" and getting married would be a good idea. Then Jason popped the question. They went house hunting and everything. But after a while, Jason stopped calling. Then he stopped coming by, and the next thing you know he broke off the engagement. Six months later, he married someone else. Jillian was devastated. She didn't go out, neglected her usual impeccable appearance, and stopped taking care of herself. Her weight noticeably crept up and her hair started to shed. Eventually, with a little help from her friends and family, Jillian started to go out once in a while, but she would try to act like the whole breakup wasn't traumatic, bothersome, or embarrassing for her. Jillian says she has moved on, but I know better. Well, you know what they say: we're all just one heartbreak away from walking in Jillian's shoes.

Sound familiar? How many times have you been out with your friends, having a mocha latte, and heard stories like this one? Change the name, the context, and a few details here and there, but these stories of heartbreak and drama remain the same—women find the loves of their lives, and then learn that he is already married, or perhaps there is a job, a hobby, or something else that makes him emotionally, physically, or otherwise unavailable. Women also tell me how they have engaged in a relationship with someone and after many years find they are alone and wondering where their men are, or what she may have done or said to have driven him away. Then there are the stories of the man who refuses to commit to a relationship—he likes things the way they are. Mysteriously, after an abrupt and unexplained breakup, that same man who said he couldn't commit later marries someone else. And the woman he left is feeling angry, bitter, and overwhelmed by self-doubt, low self-esteem, and a host of other threats to her sense of well-being. This array of converging emotional challenges often comes about because women typically have very little latitude for expression of sincere and deeply held feelings without being judged or stereotyped. Most women suppress their feelings, hold their heads up, and continue on with their lives. Unfortunately, stifling these feelings can be detrimental to a woman's physical and emotional health and overall quality of life and can lead to what I call Post-Dramatic Relationship Syndrome or PDRS.

This term is not to be confused with posttraumatic stress disorder (PTSD), which is a very serious psychiatric problem that can occur following the direct experience with or the witnessing of a traumatic, potentially life-threatening event. People who suffer from PTSD often relive the traumatic experience through nightmares and flashbacks, have difficulty sleeping, and feel detached or estranged from friends and loved ones. These symptoms can be severe enough and last long enough to significantly impair the person's daily life. The disorder also affects a person's ability to function in social situations or family life and often results in occupational instability as well as marital and family problems. Persons suffering from this disorder require and should seek professional help.

On the other hand, PDRS is not a condition officially recognized by the American Psychiatric Association (APA) and is not listed in the APA's *Diagnostic and Statistical Manual of Mental Disorders*. I coined this term to refer to the drama in our relationships and to describe the ways in which we are affected when a relationship ends. Truth be told, we all have a little drama in our relationships—a heated argument, miscommunication, differences of opinion—and these interactions are not all bad. Sometimes these experiences have psychologically positive outcomes, and they often help strengthen our relationships. The type of drama I'm referring to goes beyond the day-to-day miscommunication and involves constant upheavals that create emotional distress and imbalance. Intense disagreements, blatant deceit, and dishonesty constitute some of the interactions that turn what may once have been a mutually satisfying relationship into a frustrating and disheartening exchange of hurtful words and negative emotions. Even a significant one-time event played out in dramatic fashion can create emotional or spiritual imbalance. Such events are often unpredictable, unexpected, and sometimes unpreventable. Remember Jillian? She thought there was something she could have done to keep Jason from leaving. It was inconceivable to her that one day she would be thinking about her life with Jason and the next day he was telling her of the life he was planning with someone else. She never expected to be deceived by Jason and was deeply hurt and traumatized by this realization. She refused to accept that the relationship was really over and believed that Jason would come back to her. And that's when the drama began. After the breakup, Jillian frequently checked her text messages, caller ID, and e-mail inbox. Jillian maintained her usual routine, figuring at some point Jason would show up. But when she realized that Jason had truly left her, she called him repeatedly during the day. It didn't stop there. She went by his job and to restaurants they frequented together in the hope that he might be there. And when Jillian finally caught up with Jason at his job, she angrily confronted him at first and then changed her tone and pleaded with him to tell her what she had done wrong and to give their relationship another chance. Of course, this display of emotions gave Jason the justification he needed to walk away from her, giving bystanders the impression that *he* was the lucky one to be getting away from this obviously unstable woman. Jillian went home feeling dejected and embarrassed. She resolved not to love again.

While acceptance of a relationship's end may feel like the worst is over, it's important to be aware that the aftermath of a dramatic relationship experience can be as painful and bewildering as the relationship itself. Some women manage to go about their daily routines or may even find new relationships. It's usually not long, though, before their momentum is interrupted. Two, three, or six months later, or even a year, something triggers a memory and the emotions start flooding back. Overwhelmed by the rush of these emotions, many women find themselves in a quandary as to what to do and wonder how they can keep it together when everything seems to be unraveling. How a woman copes with all of the feelings, thoughts, and behaviors that stem from a dramatic relationship experience determines the extent to which she is at risk for PDRS.

So to be clear, there are no clinical treatments, therapies, or medications to formally address PDRS. If you have truly experienced or witnessed a traumatic event like intimate partner violence or other forms of domestic violence, please seek professional help. There is a variety of resources, hotlines, and support services available to help you or someone you know. But as we look at PDRS, this is your opportunity to acknowledge that the drama in your relationship is indeed overwhelming and is causing you distress. Dealing with the drama after a relationship has ended is even more unsettling—especially if, like Jillian, you didn't see it coming. Don't be embarrassed by it. You'll feel better once you can identify the signs and symptoms of PDRS, which you'll learn in the next chapter. Dealing with the after effects of dramatic relationships requires a good deal of steadfastness. Resolve to care enough about yourself to get the support you need when you're distressed and feeling the urge to react in ways harmful to your well-being. Resolve to surround yourself with people who will care about you, tell you the truth, and stand by you even when you might not be so easy to be around.

Finally, resolve to break the cycle of engaging in one dramatic relationship after another. Sometimes women are drawn to drama and create situations that stir up the drama in their lives because they have never experienced living in a drama-free zone. A goal of this book is to help you understand why you make the same relationship choices over and over again and why you experience PDRS and its symptoms and warning signs. The humorous anecdotes and opportunities for reflection will help you achieve personal and spiritual renewal. You'll be able to discern when you are at risk and take steps toward restoring your spiritual and emotional health. You will improve the quality of your life while having a laugh or two on the road to recovery!

CHAPTER 1

The Science of Love and Why We Do the Things We Do

BEFORE WE DELVE into PDRS, let's briefly explore the science of love. Yes! There is actually a scientific explanation for how we love and react to challenges in our relationships. Love is often understood as a powerful feeling that comes over us when we meet that special someone. A strong emotion and powerful force, love gives us a feeling of being on top of the world—it drives our behavior, clouds our thinking, and influences our judgment. The old adage "love made me do it" is the fallback justification we use when we find ourselves in uncharacteristic situations or doing things that, when in full possession of our faculties, we would never do. Yes. We seem powerless under the influence of love. Why is it that we make good decisions in our daily lives as professionals, entrepreneurs, and ordinary citizens, but have difficulty thinking and sometimes behaving rationally when it comes to love? It doesn't seem to matter if we are rich or poor, famous or not so well known, young or old, love affects all of us in beautiful and sometimes mysterious ways. We all have succumbed to its power.

Love isn't just an emotion that we experience when we find the object of our affection. It is an inextricable part of our physiological make-up and involves a wonderful interplay of a host of chemicals that when released into the body send signals to the brain affecting how we feel and what we do.[1] In fact, love has its origin in our evolutionary biology. It is nature's way of keeping the human species alive by encouraging bonding between mates and ensuring the important caregiving bond between mother and child.[2] So it's no wonder that we feel such a flood of feelings and emotions in our relationships. It is in our very nature to love, and it affects our total being in delightful and inexplicable ways. In fact, some researchers suggest that the process of falling in love activates centers in our brain in much the same way as addictions or mental-health issues such as obsessive compulsive disorder.[3] Remember that "like-a-teenager" feeling the first time you met your love interest? Do you recall how difficult it was to express yourself intelligently on your first date? How about that strange mix of emotions—warmth, elation, loss of appetite, nervousness, anxiety—all working together at the same time? Well, these experiences are all due to the cocktail of pleasure chemicals being released into your body as you embark on the magical journey of falling in love. Scientists say the process unfolds in three phases: passion, attraction, and attachment.

Let's start with the strong passion and the intense desire that overtake us when we make a connection with a potential romantic partner. Hormones such as testosterone and estrogen play significant roles in fueling lustful passion and fantasies. From a biological standpoint, these feelings prime us for intimacy and send signals to the prospective love interest that we are physically and psychologically attracted and ready to explore!

During the attraction phase, we have honed in on our intended, weeding out less desirable partners. At this point, all we see is perfection: great personality, sense of humor, good looks, charm. You name it, he's got it. He can do no wrong. One explanation for this rose-colored view of our love interest is that the chemicals in the brain associated with judgment are suppressed during this phase, supporting the notion that love is indeed blind! To complicate matters even further, chemicals such as adrenaline, which are associated with increased heart rate and stress reduction, and other chemicals associated with blissfulness, heighted attention, short-term memory, and sleeplessness are all released into the body and affect the regions of the brain regulating these processes. Do you recall experiencing a time when you couldn't eat or sleep because you couldn't stop thinking about that perfect person of your dreams? With this exciting and complex mix of chemicals affecting the way we think and behave, it's no wonder we feel confused and a little beside ourselves when falling in love. These feelings are biologically driven and together they pave the way for long-term relationships and, potentially, a lasting bond of attachment—the third phase.

This phase is associated with an overall sense of well-being and contentment and the warmth and fulfillment of attachment—what we think of as true love. A chemical called oxytocin (often called the love hormone) gives us that warm and fuzzy feeling when we are close to and have intimacy with our partner. Its purpose is to promote a strong attachment bond, ideally ensuring a long-lasting relationship. Most of the research on oxytocin focuses on the bond between mother and child; however, more recently, researchers are discovering that oxytocin plays an important role in reducing anxiety and stress. This may explain why we trust and feel safe revealing our true selves to our partners during this phase. Another chemical, vasopressin, is also associated with the long-term bond and together with endorphins produces a sense of warmth, well-being, and even peacefulness and security. The more intimacy in the relationship, the stronger the attachment bond, biologically speaking.

Biology continues to play a role as we settle into the comfort of our relationships. The intensity of passion, love blindness, and obsession subsides as the attachment and sense of security in our relationship strengthen. These changes allow us to rationally judge our partner and have a more balanced view of his strengths and weaknesses. Most importantly, the strength of the attachment bond allows us to confidently work through difficult issues that arise in the relationship, and the love chemicals allow us to still feel a sense of well-being and happiness—although now the feeling of euphoria might take a little more work and commitment to achieve.

So it's not hard to imagine that when a relationship goes awry during any one of the three phases, people experience both physical and emotional symptoms. In fact, researchers who study how the brain works in love and attraction say that emotional and physical pain are indeed connected and share pathways in the brain. So when we experience a breakup, the brain sends signals telling our body that the breakup actually hurts![4]

The way we respond to a breakup may be a reflection of how we generally react to stress and drama in our daily lives. So if we binge on comfort food when we feel stressed or depressed, have difficulty sleeping, or have trouble concentrating, some of these same challenges may be experienced in the aftermath of a breakup. One of the reasons we may find it difficult to move on after a breakup is because the chemicals released in the body during the process of falling in love act like a drug to the brain. So when a relationship ends abruptly or in a dramatic fashion, the body may actually feel like it is experiencing a withdrawal. The longer the relationship and the stronger the *perception* of the attachment, the more challenging the withdrawal and the more susceptible a person is to experiencing PDRS. In time, the brain will readjust to a new normal and soon will allow the wonder of love to be experienced again. In the next chapter, we'll focus on self-awareness and learn how to identify the signs and symptoms of PDRS.

CHAPTER 2

Take the PDRS Checkup: Know the Signs and Symptoms

IN THE INTRODUCTION, I talked about the dramatic experiences that lead to PDRS. Negative events that abruptly break the relationship bond leave you feeling spiritually and emotionally overwhelmed, especially if you did not have an opportunity for closure. Because these events are often unpredictable, unexpected and sometimes unpreventable, you may not even be aware of their impact on your emotional and spiritual well-being, not to mention your behavior. Unfortunately, friends are not always discerning enough or willing to tell you that your behavior is out of character or drastically different and disturbing. Even if they are willing, you may not be ready to hear what they have to say. You know how it is. Rather than confront you or upset you, your friends and family avoid certain topics of conversation because they don't know how you'll respond or they stop talking when you enter the room. Sound familiar?

This chapter will help you avoid the pitfalls that come with lack of self-awareness—an important factor in PDRS. You will learn how to give yourself a PDRS checkup to determine how much you have been affected by the negative events in your relationships. The checkup will help sharpen your intuition so that you know when you're experiencing an imbalance. This is important because the impact of a dramatic relationship experience can be so severe that you may not even realize what has happened to you. You say things and act in ways that are generally out of character, but feel you have no control over your behavior. This is because there may be certain stimuli in your environment that trigger an emotional impulse to respond in a certain way. You react to prompts in your environment, but you may not know what they are or what propels you into an emotional tailspin. You start your day with a sunny disposition, but somehow at day's end you're exhausted and left wondering why you feel drained or in a poor mood.

Knowing the signs and symptoms of PDRS can help you identify some of the triggers that bring on unhealthy attitudes and behaviors. To heighten your sense of self-awareness, you must first take the PDRS checkup. I have listed three major symptoms of PDRS and their accompanying attitudes and behaviors to help determine whether you're at risk. Before you take the checkup, find a quiet place where you won't be disturbed. Reflect on your thoughts and actions over the past few months since your breakup. Review each PDRS symptom and its accompanying signs. Rate each sign from one to five. A rating of one is low, meaning that this is probably not a sign of PDRS that has a consequential effect on your emotional state. A rating of three is in the mid-range. It should elevate your level of concern, but not overly so. You experience these feelings or exhibit these behaviors once in a while, but you're aware of it, and you manage to keep it under control. A rating of five means that this is a sign of PDRS that has your emotions in full throttle. You exhibit these behaviors most of the time, and you are not in control.

Are you ready for your checkup? Be honest. Don't give yourself a positive rating when you know you've been staking out his house and writing down the license-plate numbers of all of his female visitors!

⌒⟶

Symptom One: Women who suffer from PDRS relive their dramatic relationship through flashbacks and have unresolved emotions.

⌒⟶

A breakup can be a very distressing and anxiety-producing experience, particularly if it was unexpected or if the timing of the breakup was inappropriate and left you feeling embarrassed. Consequently, such dramatic events may result in a host of unresolved feelings and emotions that are difficult to sort through. You have that I-can't-get-him-out-of-my-mind fixation. You are consumed with thoughts of your ex and even your dreams are filled with recollections of the relationship you once had and perhaps wish you still had. You keep thinking that if you had done something differently or paid more attention to him, you might still be together. If you were prettier, younger, or shapelier, maybe he would have chosen you over her. The signs associated with this symptom of PDRS reflect your unconscious thoughts and behavior. So you're at risk for PDRS if you exhibit the behaviors listed in the chart below.

Signs	Rating				
	1 Never	2 Rarely	3 Sometimes	4 Often	5 Very Often
1. Get angry every time you see an "older" man with a "younger" woman.					
2. Feel angry or depressed when you observe seemingly happy couples and find reasons to criticize them.					
3. Feel sad when you order a meal you enjoyed sharing with him at your favorite restaurant.					
4. Avoid visiting a familiar place that you once frequented as a couple.					
5. Become entranced and then enraged every time you hear his name.					
6. Start talking about your ex in the middle of an unrelated conversation.					
7. Think you see your ex when you're shopping at the mall. You run to speak to him and call his name, but he doesn't answer—it's not him!					

⌒

Symptom Two: Women who suffer from PDRS may feel disconnected or experience a sense of drifting away from family and friends.

⌒

Maintaining healthy relationships requires considerable time and attention. In a dramatic relationship, you focus *all* of your time and attention on him. You often turn down opportunities to go out with your friends, visit family members, or participate in work-related or civic activities. Your whole world revolved around the "love of your life" and now that he is gone you find it difficult to move beyond the world you and he created and get reconnected with people outside of that world. The signs associated with this symptom have to do with your sense of place and belonging. So you may be experiencing PDRS if you exhibit the behaviors listed in the chart below.

Signs	Rating				
	1 Never	2 Rarely	3 Sometimes	4 Often	5 Very Often
1. Feel embarrassed by the thought that *everybody-knows-my-business*. As a result, you shy away from friends and other people you know.					
2. Want to call your friends to talk about what has happened to your relationship, but you realize that the only friends you have are the ones in your ex's social circle.					
3. Can't focus. You experience out-of-body sensations—you can see and hear people talking, but you can't engage in the conversation. Your day-to-day life feels more like a movie than reality.					
4. Have difficulty concentrating at work, in prayer, and in conversations with others.					
5. Feel a sense of being alone in the world even though you are surrounded by friends and family.					
6. Turn down offers to go to social or business events because you don't have an escort or date.					
7. Feel guilty about the *just-because-you-don't-have-a-man* attitude you once had toward your single friends. Now that your relationship is over, you act indifferent about the break-up in public, and then go home and cry yourself to sleep at night.					

Symptom Three: Women who suffer from PDRS are often unable to engage in trusting relationships with others.

Because we share so much of ourselves in relationships, especially in long-term partnerships, a dramatic or sudden breakup can deeply challenge a person's confidence. This may lead to self-doubt, self-pity, and ultimately withdrawal from social situations. You have a strong desire to protect yourself and therefore may feel guarded and have difficulty trusting. The signs associated with this PDRS symptom have to do with the conscious thoughts and behaviors related to social interaction and engagement.

So you may be at risk for PDRS if you exhibit the behaviors listed in the chart below.

Signs	Rating				
	1 Never	2 Rarely	3 Sometimes	4 Often	5 Very Often
1. You only talk about "safe" topics with your friends and deliberately change the subject when they suggest you start dating again.					
2. You meet a really nice man, but you're afraid to go out with him because you think the relationship might end up like the last one.					
3. Your friends set you up on a promising blind date, but you have a panic attack and can't get up the nerve to go inside the restaurant. So you run back to your car and hyperventilate.					
4. You increase your hours and responsibilities at work to avoid social situations.					
5. You think every guy you meet is either no good, or up to no good, so you lump them all in the "men-are-dogs" category and treat them accordingly.					

Now you might say that everyone experiences these symptoms from time to time and is tempted, once in a while, to do some of these things. Does that mean that everyone suffers from PDRS? No, of course not. But these are behavior patterns that could spiral out of control and put you on a path toward spiritual and emotional distress. Once this distress takes hold of your life, it affects your daily decision making and your interactions with others. That's why it's really important to face these issues directly. Do you ever wonder why some women seem to choose the same man over and over again? Some of the bad relationship decisions we make are the effects of PDRS unexamined. So if those edgy thoughts are more than just fleeting notions and if you find that you are consumed with unhealthy emotions or exhibiting out-of-character behaviors, you may be experiencing PDRS. Now you have the language to help clarify why you feel and behave the way you do. By acknowledging that you are truly experiencing these difficulties, you are taking the first steps toward relief from distress.

Let's revisit your checkup. If you gave yourself an honest appraisal of your thoughts and actions, you should have a range of responses to the signs and symptoms. If you have a good deal of ones and twos, this suggests that you have a relatively healthy perspective, given what you've experienced. I encourage you to check yourself regularly. Why? Sometimes reactions to these events may not manifest right away. Also, meditate daily, stay socially connected, and maintain a strong support system so that you can talk with a trusted friend if you start to feel overwhelmed or find yourself exhibiting strange behavior in social situations.

If your behavior falls somewhere in the middle and you have given yourself a good deal of threes on your checkup, you probably have supports in place to keep you grounded. Occasionally, however, you may teeter a little to the left or to the right. It will be really important for you to stay connected to close family and friends and to get involved in philanthropic, community, or other activities to keep you socially engaged and emotionally and spiritually balanced.

Finally, if you have given yourself more fours and fives than you thought you would, this suggests that the nature of your relationship and subsequent breakup affected you deeply and that you are indeed experiencing the signs and symptoms of PDRS. There are some things you need to do right now. First, forgive yourself, and acknowledge that it's alright to feel the way you do. Even if there are things in the relationship you wish you hadn't said (like calling him emasculating names) or you wish you hadn't done (like auctioning off his suits on eBay), blaming yourself is not going to change the situation. Raise your right hand and repeat after me: "He is not coming back!" We all have fallen short from time to time in our efforts to make relationships work and, yes, it does hurt and disappoint when things don't work out. But while you're hurting, take the time to learn the signs and symptoms of PDRS. Know that you're not alone in the way you feel or are tempted to behave. Soon all of things that you are going through now will be a memory. But what you choose to remember—positive experiences that helped you to grow spiritually and emotionally or moments of anger and resentment—is entirely up to you. Which path will you choose?

You are not the only person I want you to forgive. Your next step is to forgive him. I know this is a tall order, especially if he clearly set out to deceive or take advantage of you. The ability to forgive is a gift from God, and the act of forgiveness is more for you than it is for him. Acknowledge your hurt, release it, and let it go. Recall those words, phrases, and labels he used that really cut to the core of your soul. Write them down on separate pieces of paper. While you are writing, experience what it feels like to detach yourself from those labels—you don't own those words, and they are no longer a part of you. Now put each piece of paper through the shredder. If you have a fireplace, drop them one by one into the flames. Even better, rip the papers into tiny little pieces so that you exert some physical energy in this process. Discard the residue—the ashes, the shreds, and each scrap. Observe how words that once had so much power over you are now just ashes and discarded pieces of paper. Feel the release of tension, stress, and anxiety. Now take a deep breath and feel the freedom, the peace, and the joy flooding into your spirit. Be calm. Celebrate and give thanks for this new freedom. You may not feel like celebrating right away, but it's important for you to begin acknowledging this new phase of your journey forward, especially on the physical and intellectual levels. Soon you'll experience emotional freedom, and your mind, body, and soul will be in sync.

But there's one more thing that you've got to do—and this might be the toughest of all. Get up, get dressed, and go to the coffee shop where your friends spend time. Drop in while they're having that mocha latte. Order a double latte for yourself. Sit down, look your friends in the eyes, smile, and say, "Hi, ladies. I know you heard what happened between Jason and me. I'm sorry that I've kept you at arm's length while all of this was going on, but I really appreciate your patience and your friendship. Have you heard about something called PDRS? It's not a disease or disorder, but it's the way we respond when our relationships don't quite work out. Well, that's what I was experiencing. Let me tell you about it..."

Notes and Reflections
on the Signs and Symptoms of PDRS

_____
_____
_____
_____
_____
_____
_____
_____
_____
_____
_____
_____
_____
_____
_____
_____
_____
_____
_____
_____
_____
_____
_____
_____
_____
_____
_____
_____
_____
_____

Understanding the Three Ps of Relationships

ONE OF THE reasons that relationships have such a profound impact on our lives is because we expose our most vulnerable selves to another person. Engaging with another human being on any level involves risk. Love and romance are particularly risky because we place our hopes and dreams (whether realistic or not) on the other person. And when they disappoint and that relationship falls short of realizing those dreams or fulfilling that hope, it can fuel unnecessary drama and change the dynamic of the relationship. To avoid PDRS, we need to better understand what I call the *three Ps of relationships*—the *perils*, the *promise*, and the *power*. This next section focuses on the importance of these three relationship factors to help you maintain a balanced perspective and ultimately a more fulfilling and satisfying relationship.

CHAPTER 3

The Perils of Relationships: Put on Your Protective Gear!

WE COMMONLY UNDERSTAND *peril* as being exposed to risk or harm or a source of danger. To consider the words *peril* and *relationship* together appears to be oxymoronic, especially when you're talking about them in the context of spiritual health and happiness. After all, why would someone expose herself to someone who could cause harm or put her at risk? But, in fact, that's what we are doing when we enter into a relationship—it's risky business. As discussed in chapter 1, letting someone into your heart is a vulnerable proposition that can hurt, disappoint, and yes, even cause pain—that's the stuff of relationships. In many ways, launching a new relationship is something like learning to ride a bicycle. You start off with training wheels to give you balance and support and keep you from falling over. But when the supports come off, watch out. You're vulnerable to the bumps in the road, uneven pavement, and unexpected obstacles on the sidewalk. At times you'll fall and scrape your knees and elbows, but this is all part of the process of learning to ride. You get up, dust yourself off, patch up your wounds, and climb back on the bicycle. Before you know it, the wounds have healed and you're cruising down the road on two wheels like a pro. As you gain more experience, take more chances, and challenge your new riding abilities, you might even wear protective gear like helmet, gloves, and kneepads so that when the inevitable fall comes, you're protected from possible head trauma and other major injuries. But you ride on—you've mastered the terrain and you know what you're getting into. You've prepared yourself for the perils that can come with taking on this level of challenge.

The same is true in relationships. You may ease cautiously into a new relationship and are careful not to say or reveal too much, too soon. You may have double dates or go to neutral or safe places until you have some degree of confidence that the person you're with is at least sane. Then you may go on dates without your friends to a more intimate and romantic place for dinner. Then once you feel free enough to peel back another layer of yourself and are ready to take more risks, you will begin to experience disappointments and hurts—unfortunately, these things are a part of the process too. But if there's enough trust and patience in this budding relationship, you figure out how to get beyond the bumps and scrapes and move on to the next level. The more confident you are in your relationship, the more you share and, of course, the more vulnerable you become. Where there is trust, openness, and honesty, you can strike a wonderful balance. But just like riding that bicycle, if you decide to speed up and take more risks you've got to protect yourself from the perils that will surely come. No, not with helmets, gloves, and knee pads but with the spiritual and emotional safeguards I've outlined below to help protect your heart and buffer your soul from the dramatic events that could potentially derail you and lead to PDRS.

⟵◠⟶

Recognize that relationships should be a two-way street. While you're sharing and giving, you should also be listening and receiving.

⟵◠⟶

Women are often inclined to share thoughts and feelings more readily and reflectively than men. At a given moment, we can reach down into the depths of our souls and identify the source of our joy and our pain and talk fluently and passionately about why we feel the way we do. Often we dominate the discussions with our insights, so much so that we fail to realize that we're the only one talking! Give your partner a chance to share what's important to him and what's on his mind—his dreams and aspirations, likes and dislikes. And when he does, please listen. What he has to share will reveal plenty about who he is and what he is capable of giving in the relationship. He might not say these things directly, or with the same level of clarity, reflection, or even thoughtfulness as you do, but be patient and respectful and listen with an open mind and heart. Be sure to tune in to his nonverbal language as well—what he doesn't say can also speak volumes. Is he responsive to you when you share your thoughts and feelings? Does he at least appear to be moved and empathetic by the things that move you, give you joy, or cause you pain? He may not necessarily understand your feelings or even agree with them, and that's alright. What's important here is whether there is enough chemistry between the two of you that he feels compelled to share in both the joys and the challenges you experience. In other words, the things that matter to you should matter to him. Indeed, *you* matter to him. You should be able to discern from the sincerity (or lack thereof) of his words and his verbal and nonverbal behavior if the relationship has turned onto a one-way street and is headed toward a dead end.

At the same time, you need to be tuned in to his feelings and thoughts. What makes his heart sing? What affects him deeply? If he senses that the things that matter to him don't matter to you, then he might not be so responsive the next time you want to pour out your soul. So if you want to avoid the perils of a one-way-street relationship, you have to be willing to give and receive, to share and to listen.

Don't be so quick to make excuses for your partner—let his actions speak for themselves and then behave accordingly.

Women are nurturers by design. We are equipped with the ability to give, nurture, and sustain life until that life can sustain itself. In the process, we protect and shield from harm. We wipe the tears away, kiss the hurt, and make it all better. In parental relationships, this nurturing helps strengthen a child's sense of self and gives him or her the confidence to go out and face the world with all of its challenges. The innate capacity to nurture is a gift with which most women are endowed. However, we often extend this wonderful gift into our adult relationships with men. We *understand* when he fails to remember a date, your birthday, or other significant event, and we *willingly pay* his way when he's "a little short this month." We do these things in part because we know life is tough—especially for men of color who may not have careers or jobs that allow them to have much flexibility with their time and resources. Because society rarely gives them a break, we think we should do so by nurturing them and sheltering them from life's storms. That's fine as long as the ground rules are clear. Otherwise, there will be consequences when he realizes that you actually don't have ground rules and that you're not going to hold him to a high standard of behavior. He's likely to start taking you for granted, and in response, you suppress your anger because you don't want to lose him. I'm sorry to say that if it has gotten to this point, you may have already lost him. Please don't make excuses for his behavior. If he's consistently late for your dates and scheduled plans, what does that say about how he values your time? Most importantly, what do his actions say about how important you are to him? If a business associate or client always kept you waiting, you'd cancel the contract or fire the associate—right? Time is a valuable commodity, don't let anyone waste yours. Don't react by yelling and telling him off—just cancel the contract. Make yourself available for someone who will value you, your time, and all that you have to offer. But you won't connect with that person if you're sitting at home waiting for the one who has no time for you. These are a few ground rules to help you get started:

Always remain true to yourself. Know your threshold for compassion. If it feels more like you are mothering than engaging in a responsible adult relationship, then start letting him be accountable for his behavior. You don't have to overextend yourself to be loved. You're worthy of being loved just because of who you are. There's an old saying that you teach people how to treat you by the way you behave and the way you respond to their behaviors. You don't have to come to his rescue every time he has a wrinkle or tussle in his life. These things are not your responsibility. Fixing is not your role. His mother did that for him a long time ago.

Distinguish between reasonable and unreasonable requests. If what he is asking feels like an imposition, it probably is. On the other hand, if what he is asking you to do is the least of what you would do for any of your friends, then by all means respond affirmatively. Just keep in mind that there are limits.

Determine whether there are opportunities for reciprocity. You're not expecting a tit for tat here, but you do want to feel confident in the mutuality of your relationship. Is he willing to wait for you? Is he unforgiving when you have to cancel a date?

Unrealistic relationship expectations will lead you down the slippery slope to PDRS.

If you think that having a man will solve your problems, you'll definitely need to put on full protective gear and brace yourself for a fall! I know you've heard this a million times, but I'll say it again for good measure: no one can meet all of your needs. This is by far the most common peril of relationships. You breathe a sigh of relief when he comes into your life, and you expect all of your fantasies and notions about relationships to come to fruition through this one man. You've just set yourself up for disappointment. He's not a knight in shining armor who was sent to rescue you or make all of your dreams come true. In fact, he doesn't own armor, and he can't even ride a horse! So give the guy some breathing room. Expect from him what first and foremost relationships are designed to provide—friendship and companionship. The hallmarks of true friendship are mutual respect and trust. Does your behavior convey to him that he can trust you—and vice versa? Do you respect him for the values he holds? Are those values reflected in the choices he makes? Do you carry yourself in such a way that compels him to respect you? Does he know the values that are deeply written in your heart? Answers to these questions reflect what I call your friendship quotient. Sit down with your partner and talk about the "friendship" in your relationship. Spend time establishing that part of your relationship first and then maybe he'll agree to take horseback-riding lessons!

The Friendship Quotient

Is he someone you'd spend time with if you didn't have romantic interests?

A. Yes   B. No   C. I'm not sure

Is your interest in him contingent upon his money, and/or perceived status?

A. Yes   B. No   C. I'm not sure

What is the nature of <u>your</u> attraction to him?

A. Purely romantic/physical   E. Professional goals
B. Personality   F. Ethical/moral values
C. Social interests/hobbies   G. I'm not sure
D. Family background

Have you introduced him to your friends?

A. Yes   B. No   C. Not Yet

What does he have in common with your other friends?

Has he introduced you to his friends?

A. Yes   B. No   C. Not yet

What do you have in common with his friends?

What is the nature of <u>his</u> attraction to you?

A. Purely romantic/physical   E. Professional goals
B. Personality   F. Ethical/moral values
C. Social interests/hobbies   G. I'm not sure
D. Family background

CHAPTER 4

The Promise of Relationships: Where Hope Resides

DESPITE THE INEVITABLE perils of relationships, women remain hopeful. We desire caring, committed relationships and believe that no matter what, love is still possible. This is the promise of relationships. It is the belief that despite whatever happened in the past, history doesn't have to be repeated. You believe you will find a relationship in which you can have confidence and a sense of belonging, well-being, and pride. Yes, you still hope for the childhood fairy tale of Prince Charming coming on a white horse to whisk you away. Or you hope to find the lonely widower who, like Tom Hanks in *Sleepless in Seattle*, just needs a little push to get out there again in the dating game before finding his soul mate. You hope that the successful business tycoon will realize that all of his accomplishments and all of his wealth mean nothing without someone like you to share it with. And yes, you hope that somewhere a perfectly fashioned man is out there looking and waiting for you. Somehow he will find you—the woman of his dreams. Someday your paths will cross.

This kind of hopefulness is really important and serves as a protective buffer against PDRS. When the stress and drama of relationships past and present challenge and threaten your sense of well-being, it's really important to find a place in your heart where true hope resides. True hope is born out of a deep, abiding faith that all things are possible and that you have the capacity to love and give of yourself in a healthy way. The failures of your past relationships do not disqualify you from having a satisfying relationship in the future. Some women mask hope in an "I don't care—if it happens, it happens" attitude and bury themselves in their work and family affairs or make social causes their singular focus. Other women are quietly hopeful, afraid to let their hope shine through for fear of what others might think or say about them. Still others just move on with a broken heart, counting on time and enough distance to heal their wounds. These behaviors are detrimental not only to your future prospect of finding love, but to your physical, spiritual, and emotional health. Holding on to negative energy disguised as resilience is problematic because that energy has to go somewhere. Often the negative energy manifests itself physically—breaking down our immune systems or affecting our eating habits or sleeping patterns. Women of color are disproportionately affected by chronic conditions such as obesity, hypertension, and diabetes. While a direct link has not been established between relationship quality and these conditions, it is important to be aware that the cumulative effect of one dramatic relationship after another may bring on the kind of stress associated with these chronic diseases. If you feel overly tired, have difficulty sleeping, and either have no appetite or eat excessively, you must determine the source of these problems. Check with your doctor or mental health provider first. If these are not pre-existing medical conditions, you might be suffering from symptoms of PDRS.

In a similar way, hope protects against PDRS. How? Hope brings on a level of optimism that fosters spiritual and emotional equilibrium. You send out positive energy that signals to others that you're open, available, and willing to live in the moment and experience life. The ultimate promise of relationships is that someone wonderful will recognize the qualities of your heart and the essence of your soul and that together new treasures of the heart and soul will be discovered. So to obtain the promise of relationships, here are a few things that you can do today:

Start and end your day with positive affirmations from your favorite scripture or inspirational book. Write them down. Say them out loud. Find at least one person to share those affirmations with daily. Start an affirmations club and make a commitment to encourage, inspire, and uplift others.

Stay active. If you don't have a regular exercise routine, start your day by moving to your favorite music. In no time at all, you'll be working up a sweat and working out your anger, anxieties, and apprehensions about relationships.

Keep a daily record of what you eat. Are you consuming foods that are healthy or foods laden with fat, sugar, and salt that make you feel tired, bloated, and weighed down? As you record your food intake, also take note of how you feel before and after you eat and the events or activities that have occurred before you eat. The more aware you are of what, when, and why you eat, the more you'll be motivated to replace foods that sap your energy and enthusiasm with healthy foods that help fuel hope and optimism.

Have a least one good belly laugh a day. This is my motto. I love to laugh. Laughter is wonderful medicine for the heart and soul. It also has been associated with positive health benefits. So at the end of a long, hard day, find humor in your interactions with your colleagues and co-workers. Reflect on relationship interactions past and present and enjoy a side-splitting, eye-watering round of laughter.

CHAPTER 5

The Power of Relationships: Maintaining a Healthy Balance

RELATIONSHIPS ARE THE cornerstone of human life. There is no greater influence on our development than the power of the one-to-one connection between human beings. Positive relationships at the earliest point in our lives are the foundation for success in later relationships. Throughout life, we strive for relationships and connections that will assure us, make us feel safe, bring confidence, and boost our sense of self. Relationships are so central to our well-being that people will do whatever it takes to find a mutually satisfying experience. In fact, our survival depends on it. That's why it hurts so deeply when relationships fail. To avoid the hurt, women in particular will overextend themselves and put forth their best effort to keep even a detrimental and dramatic relationship intact. The results, though, can be devastating, creating an imbalance of power in the relationship and setting women up for PDRS.

This power imbalance happens in a number of ways. First, the person who desires the relationship most relinquishes the power. That's because that person wants the relationship so badly that she will do anything to keep it in tact. That means that you are always going to work harder, give more, and ask for less in this relationship because it's what *you* want. Remember riding the seesaw as a kid? In many ways, the seesaw is a metaphor for relationship power. There is a long, solid plank with seats on both ends and handlebars to prevent you from falling and toppling over. In the middle, there's a fulcrum that allows the long wooden plank to balance evenly when the weight of the person on each end is relatively equal. One person gets the ride going by pushing off with her feet, and the other person, if heavy enough, pulls the plank down on his side, allowing you to ride high for a while. The other person pushes off with his feet, and your weight pulls the plank down on your side. The back and forth of this kind of ride allows you to experience the euphoria of riding high, the grounded reality of pulling your side down, and the delicateness of bringing your weight to balance. However, if the other person is not heavy enough, no matter how much you push, you never quite get off the ground. If the person is too heavy, you're left to dangle in the air, and you never get your feet on the ground. Worst of all, if the person abruptly gets off the seesaw while you're in the air, you rapidly plunge down to the ground and hit the surface with a traumatic impact. Relationship power is like this. Too much or too little effort on one side or the other creates an imbalance and can lead to a rough landing. If there is no real commitment, a relationship can end abruptly, causing a tremendous amount of trauma that can lead to PDRS. Trust is what keeps the relationship in balance and, working together with friendship and love, determines whether you'll survive the ups and downs or whether your relationship will hit rock bottom.

Second, the power imbalance in a relationship happens when you're not fully honest about who you are and what matters most to you. You relinquish your power by not being totally honest with your partner—by not expressing your likes or dislikes, not being willing to be vulnerable but always covering up with the "strong woman persona" or being defensive about your weaknesses. What I mean by power is not dominance—*(If violence is occurring in your relationship or if you feel threatened or fearful, please tell someone close to you and seek help.)*— but it is the full capacity you have to explore, discover, learn together, grow together, hurt together, give and receive love.

The drama in a relationship occurs when your partner begins to treat you according to the way you present yourself in the relationship. For example, if you always act like a helpless woman in need of rescuing and attention, then he will treat you like someone who has no capacity to solve her own problems. If you always act like a strong, invincible woman whose heart is surrounded by a fortress and is fortified by previous hurt, suspicion, and distrust, he will treat you with resistance as well. As a result, he could either retreat from doing battle with you or will use whatever ammunition he has to protect himself. In the end, this situation is bound to create bad feelings, and you will experience PDRS because you feel like he didn't really give you a chance—he got off the seesaw abruptly. To put the relationship back in balance, you tell him you'll change or you begin to peel away some of the thick, protective layers surrounding your heart. But this is difficult to do, and it often takes a great deal of time and patience for both you and your partner to achieve harmony. If there is a solid plane of love and friendship, you can then ride through the highs and lows until you reach a delicate balance. This is what you can do to re-establish the balance of power in a relationship:

Re-establish your bond of attachment. Watch how a mother lovingly interacts with her baby and do the same with your partner. You don't always have to talk; you can just gaze into each other's eyes, looking as if you can see into the soul. Get familiar with the sound of each other's voice—not just the audible voice but the inner voice that speaks quietly about the qualities of the heart and soul. Gently touch each other. Also explore the curves and contours of each other's body as if you desire to heal, calm, and soothe. But don't be so quick to rush to intimacy. If you do, you'll tip the balance of power again.

Be present in the relationship. Watch a well-bonded couple and see how the obvious contrasts in their personalities seem to work together synergistically. They have a relationship that is balanced and based on trust. They have grown to know each other intimately and, as a result, are willing to be emotionally available, to be vulnerable, and to be strong. They have taught themselves how to treat each other by behaving in ways that are true to who they are, not who they think the other person wants them to be.

Notes and Reflections
on the Three Ps of Relationships

_____
_____
_____
_____
_____
_____
_____
_____
_____
_____
_____
_____
_____
_____
_____
_____
_____
_____
_____
_____
_____
_____
_____
_____
_____
_____
_____
_____
_____

We Are Every Woman: Embrace the Sisterhood

IN SECTION 1, we found Jillian really struggling with PDRS. Jillian loved and she lost. Unfortunately, in the process she alienated her family and friends as she focused all of her attention on Jason. When Jillian's friends tried to warn her that she might be in over her head, she accused them of being jealous of her relationship. This was Jillian's ready defense: "I'm not like you, and besides, I can change him."

Of course, now we know that Jillian underestimated her ability to change Jason. In the previous section, we learned that the power of relationships is not based on your ability to change your partner or whether you can change yourself for him. Rather, the power to change lies in whether you have the strength to be yourself and allow your partner to be who he is. Doing so means that the two of you can discover, change, and grow together. Assuming that she was somehow different from every other woman is where Jillian went wrong. She thought, "Jason picked me from among all the other women, so there must be something unique and special about me, right?" On some level, Jillian is correct. People are naturally drawn to others because they see some complementary part of themselves in their love interest. This is the basis of attraction. However, once a connection is made and you begin spending time together, he'll recognize the ways—good, bad, or indifferent—in which you are similar to other women he has encountered in his life. That's human nature. There are elements of every woman in all of us. So when one of us suffers from PDRS, it affects every person in our friendship circle and makes us think about how relationships have affected our own spiritual and emotional health. We are all connected to each other through the experiences and bond of womanhood.

In the next few chapters, you'll be introduced to composites of women that I created to illustrate how our experiences and the decisions we make at different stages of life have an impact on our well-being. When you read the descriptions of each woman, you might think of women you know or be reminded of experiences you had at some point along your journey. You'll laugh a little, cry a little, and even feel a little uncomfortable, but take it all in stride and follow the reflection activities at the end of each chapter. When you are done with your personal reflection, share your thoughts and insights with your sister-friends.

CHAPTER 6

Estealla—On a Mission to Steal a Man

MEET ESTEALLA. SHE'S young, bright, ambitious, and beautiful—with every hair in place, nails done, makeup impeccable. Estealla attended the right schools and is trying hard to land her dream job. She is also channeling her energy into snagging the "right" man. Estealla is in hot pursuit of the one she believes will complement her life and provide the things that she is accustomed to having (or would like to have). In business and in love, Estealla is working on a tight timeline for the things that she wants to accomplish. She has a business plan with corporate milestones and a personal plan with a list of all the qualities and attributes she would like to see in a man. People are immediately impressed when they meet her. She is intelligent but also engaging and approachable. Estealla is on a mission. She knows what she has going for her, and she uses her charisma to open doors and network with corporate partners. If there is an important event happening, Estealla is sure to be there with her signature strong handshake. She looks her prospects in the eyes when she meets them and before they ask "how can I reach you?" Estealla has already sent a friend request on social media. When an opportunity presents itself in business or in love, she takes it even if someone gets hurt in the process. Estealla doesn't intentionally seek to take what doesn't belong to her, but after all she is on the fast track and has goals to meet. Her energy, drive, and enthusiasm are captivating and can leave you breathless and bit envious. Estealla's whole life is ahead of her. The world is hers to conquer, and she is well on her way.

The upside for Estealla is that she is bright and ambitious. She will likely succeed in everything she does. Along the way, Estealla has been resourceful as she plans carefully for her future and the comfortable lifestyle she wants. People generally like her and she has a large network of acquaintances.

In love, she always gets her man—no matter what. The downside, though, is that she may overlook the person ideally suited for her because he may not have the appeal, glitz, and glamour she thinks she wants and needs. For her, the perfect is the enemy of the good. She pays no attention to the man who perhaps is not as credentialed as she would like or who does not attend all the right meetings or belong to the right church. In her pursuit to make all the right connections, she may take the wrong direction, follow the wrong clues, and strategize herself right out of a wonderful opportunity.

As Estealla pursues her goals, she is confronted with three possible scenarios:

(1) She'll meet Mr. Right who is also a high achiever and one of Estealla's corporate partners. They share common interests personally and professionally while maintaining the competitive edge.
(2) She'll encounter Mr. Suave, Debonair, and Married to whom she loses her soul and zest for life.
(3) Estealla will choose to stay alone because the right man with the right attributes and credentials has not yet come along.

Reflection Questions

- *Which scenario do you think Estealla will choose and why?*
- *Which of these scenarios could put Estealla in a dramatic relationship, possibly leading to PDRS?*

- *Given her drive and ambition, is there another scenario that you can envision for Estealla?*
- *Make a list of what you believe are the best of Estealla's qualities and attributes and how many you think you possess. How can you use these qualities to achieve your goals in friendship and in love?*

CHAPTER 7

Ineda—"I Need a Man, But Not Just Any Man"

THIS IS INEDA. On the surface, she is calm, collected, and together. She is successful and has accomplished much in life. Ineda is well educated, has a high-powered job, owns her own home, and has a luxury car. She did everything "right" in life. She stayed in school, landed a great job, and didn't have any consequential drama in her life. She has a solid faith that sustains her through all the trials and tribulations of achieving success. Although Ineda has worked hard and acquired nice things along the way, she has reached the stage in her life when material possessions don't matter—they don't define who she is. What matters most to Ineda are the things that money can't buy—love, friendship, and the one thing she doesn't have, companionship.

Unfortunately, Ineda has been so absorbed in her work that she has not taken the time to cultivate relationships. To the observer, it looks like she doesn't want a relationship. And because Ineda usually always looks so contented, people assume that she is satisfied with her life as it is and doesn't need anything or anybody else. Not so. Ineda has a strong desire to meet someone. Not just anyone but someone special. She is looking for her soul mate: a person on whom she can rely—someone who complements her spiritually and emotionally. But this desire has taken a back seat to her work. She pushes herself to stay on top of her game, but it's come at a cost. Her body and health have been neglected, and her personal needs are an afterthought. If her so-called biological clock is ticking at all, she doesn't hear it because she is so dedicated to her work. One day, though, Ineda wakes up and has a defining moment: she's devoted a significant portion of her life to accomplishing her career goals, but her social and personal goals have gone woefully lacking. So she regroups, puts things in perspective, refocuses, and is now just as diligent in trying to find a man—but not just any man—to round out her life.

The upside for Ineda is that she has a solid foundation of faith, and her priorities are in order. She is not looking for a man to give her things—she is truly looking for companionship. In return, Ineda will make a wonderful companion. She is funny and caring and has the personal qualities that make for a good partner. She has long since shed the list of "must-haves" that she might have required in her younger days because she has come to realize that things and people aren't always as they appear. Everyone has shortcomings. You have to make allowances for people by being patient and showing compassion. This kind of wisdom has been the hallmark of her success.

The downside for Ineda is that she has been out of touch with the social arena for so long that she needs to relearn those social skills. She is approaching middle age and has to consider her health, and yes, be aware of her biological clock—it's ticking! Now that she's awake, she doesn't know what to do next. She wonders, "Where are all the men, especially the ones my age—who are available and not married?" She also realizes that there are other women out there in the same position and searching for the same good man. How does she compete with them? What's Ineda to do?

Finding herself at a cross road, Ineda has to confront four possible scenarios:

(1) Ineda gets in the game and learns to meet, greet, and mingle with confidence and flair. Unexpectedly, she meets a high-school friend and slowly but steadily they get reacquainted.

(2) She settles for "good old Joe," who is equally accomplished, comfortable, and easy to be with but not particularly exciting. She likes him, but there's no real passion.

(3) She is romanced by "Mr. Rock Your World," but he may not have her best interest at heart—moving the relationship along much faster than Ineda's comfort level.

(4) Getting back into the game proved too overwhelming and disappointing. Ineda retreats and throws herself back into her work.

Reflection Questions

- *Which of these scenarios do you think Ineda will choose and what might be the relationship perils she could experience? Which do you think might land her in a dramatic relationship that could lead to PDRS?*

- *In what ways do you identify with Ineda? Are you at a cross-road in your life? Which direction will you take? What resources or support do you need to help guide you in your decision making?*

- *Make a list of the family, friends, mentors, and acquaintances that could possibly help you re-engage socially. Organize the list according to the most and the least social. Over the next thirty days, contact the top five people on your list and make a date for a friendly get-together. Let them know your goals and ask them to send you an invitation when they host a social event.*

CHAPTER 8

Desperanza—Desperate to Find Herself and Her Man

SAY HELLO TO Desperanza. She has made her share of unfortunate decisions but has few regrets. Of course, there are things that Desperanza wishes she had done differently. But looking back on the men she has dated and the man she ultimately married, she realizes that her life has been enriched by all of these experiences. Desperanza is middle age. She has loved and lost, but she has also gained. Desperanza has children and all the responsibilities that come with being a single mom, including her share of stress and struggles.

Desperanza once had big dreams—graduate from college and work in corporate America—but they didn't happen. Her life took a different course. She got married before she finished college and had children because there was a void in her life. She felt she needed someone to complete her—to give her an identity and affirm her sense of self-worth. Desperanza thought she found what she was looking for—her savior—because he looked good and otherwise appeared to have everything she had been hoping for. But when she looked beneath the surface of his handsome and well-put-together exterior, Desperanza discovered a different, needier, less desirable man. She lived a life of making sacrifices and numerous attempts to keep the marriage together. Then she realized that she needed to leave and go her own way.

After the divorce, she struggles to get her life back on track. She finds a job that pays better than the one she had, but it's not fulfilling. Despite having a new apartment for her family and her own reliable transportation, Desperanza isn't satisfied. She feels a sense of desperation—struggling to find and release the person she was born to be, to accomplish her goals, and reach her potential. As Desperanza settles into her new life, she is intensely focused on improving herself and to her surprise, love comes again. She isn't looking for it and certainly isn't expect it. She's not even sure if she wants it, but it's real and her passion is ignited. Desperanza is desperate to maintain her sense of self and keep from getting lost again in another man's dreams. Desperanza cannot deny the promise and the power of the developing relationship.

The upside for Desperanza is that she has moved along a positive course. Now that she is in touch with who she is, Desperanza will work hard to maintain her identity while at the same time learn to share herself with a new love.

The downside for Desperanza is that she could reject love because of her fear of failing and her lack of assuredness. Out of her sense of desperation, she could alienate the very thing she is looking and praying for.

There are three possible scenarios that Desperanza could encounter:

(1) She will proceed with caution and have a balanced, healthy relationship with her new love.
(2) Her passion for life overshadows her love interest, and she foregoes the relationship to pursue her goals.
(3) Desperanza tries so hard to make the relationship work that she creates a power imbalance in the relationship. She finds herself recreating the relationship she had with her first husband.

Reflection Questions

- *Which of these scenarios do you think Desperanza will choose and why?*
- *Which do you think might land her in a dramatic relationship that could lead to PDRS?*
- *If she chooses to pursue a relationship, what can Desperanza do to establish a balance of power?*
- *What aspects of Desperanza's life and experiences do you identify with? List five things you are really passionate about. What action steps can you take to make these passions a reality?*

CHAPTER 9

Constance—The Steady, Focused, and Constant Friend

WELCOME CONSTANCE. SHE is self-assured, self-directed, and secure. She is now beyond middle age and well established in life. She is a widow, and her children are grown with lives of their own. Not quite ready to retire, Constance enjoys her life and job. She volunteers in the community and is active civically and socially. Constance has lived her life with grace and style. She is a role model who is always willing to share her wisdom and knowledge. Others gladly look to her for guidance and advice. A driven woman, Constance channels her energy and focus on what matters most in her life—friendship, family, and faith. She lives in the here and now and takes each day as it comes. She is a constant source of inspiration to her family and friends. While Constance is concerned about making life better for others, she is also hopeful that she will again find love. It's something she wants, and she shares this desire with her friends. This is not to say that she hasn't had relationships nor had her heart broken from time to time. Constance has had her share of romantic interludes since her husband passed away. Some of her relationships have been solely for companionship—someone nice to have dinner with, to call when she wants to see a movie, or to escort her to a civic dinner or gala. She can tell you stories about being pursued by seemingly well-established men. But as it turns out, some were only interested in her resources, connections, and money. After all that, Constance considers those experiences the stepping stones she needed to a new phase of love and living. She prays and meditates often and remains steadfast in her faith and resolve to maintain a balanced life—and a future of relationships with no drama.

The upside for the Constance is her steadfastness. Constance is propelled to forge ahead; she doesn't dwell in the past. She readily forgives others and is not self-aggrandizing. She is generally well liked by everyone and enjoys a strong relationship with her family. She uses her time wisely and is involved in a wide variety of clubs and activities. She travels, often spontaneously, and tries to live her life to the fullest.

The downside for Constance is that she often is overextended with so many responsibilities and projects at home, at church, and in the community. People know that they can count on Constance, even when they call on her at the last minute to give of her time and resources. Constance is so busy, so directed, and so focused that she may not see love when it comes.

There are three possible scenarios Constance could encounter:

(1) She will continue to live and enjoy her life with flair. Constance feels she will not find the kind of love she had with her late husband and is content to reflect on her memories of their life together while enjoying casual dating.
(2) Love will present itself to Constance through one of her volunteer committees, but the potential new love of her life happens to be fifteen years younger than she is.
(3) Constance will be caught off guard by love with someone she meets on one of her trips. They have a whirlwind romance, but that man will turn out to be less than trustworthy and their relationship will make Constance susceptible to PDRS.

Reflection Questions

- *Which of these scenarios do you think will happen to Constance and why? Which do you think might place Constance in a dramatic relationship that could possibly lead to PDRS?*

- *What aspects of Constance's life do you identify with?*
- *Do you attract partners who may be untrustworthy? Why?*
- *To what extent are your professional and civic activities keeping you too busy to find love? Are you using these activities to avoid finding love?*

*Notes and Reflection
on Embracing the Sisterhood*

_____
_____
_____
_____
_____
_____
_____
_____
_____
_____
_____
_____
_____
_____
_____
_____
_____
_____
_____
_____
_____
_____
_____
_____
_____
_____
_____
_____
_____
_____
_____

SECTION 4

Finding Your Drama-Free Zone

MANY OF US are drawn to dramatic relationships because we have never known what it is like to live drama-free. We have unmet needs that we look to our partners to resolve and sometimes press forward into new relationships with the heavy baggage of these unmet needs in tow. This approach leads to engaging in dramatic relationships and ultimately experiencing PDRS. This section brings together everything you've learned so far about the process for moving toward life in your drama-free zone. You'll learn how to resolve unmet needs and move closer to realizing your goals and dreams. Take some time at the end of chapter 10 to reflect on your life and lay out a plan for moving from where you are now to your drama-free zone. Share your plan with your friends and family, and build a network of people who are willing to help you follow your plan. Together make a commitment to live in *your* drama-free zone—whatever that means for you. Finally, in chapter 11 you'll find out what happened to Jillian and how she resolved her post-dramatic relationship issues.

CHAPTER 10

Resolve Unmet Needs

IN THE PREVIOUS section of this book, you were reminded of the idea that women are not one-dimensional beings and that throughout life we make decisions that allow us to grow and change. Each of the four examples illustrates how decisions we make can put us on a path to well-being or down the road to PDRS. The specific life experiences of Estealla, Ineda, Desperanza, and Constance are very different, but their basic needs, hopes, and desires are quite similar. The same is true for most women. We're all striving toward the goals of health, happiness, and abundance—the drama-free zone.

Movement toward these goals requires us to resolve unmet needs at every step along our journey. Trying to get beyond a dramatic relationship or to commit to a new love relationship before taking an inward look at *how* we resolve these needs might result in missteps that take us right back to the place we started.

So let's start from the beginning. The first type of need I'm referring to are the *basic needs of daily living* like food, shelter, and clothing. Addressing these needs might call for a better job with a higher salary, more suitable housing, or other necessities that will improve the quality of our life. To resolve these needs, some women seek men with money, status, or other material resources, hoping that he can help alleviate some of the pressure they may be experiencing. Finding someone with this goal in mind may temporarily ease the urgencies of material needs but, in the long run, such a relationship will prove unfulfilling and may result in a power imbalance.

It's also important to keep in mind that while wrestling with the urgencies of our needs, we sometimes assume that a man's offers to help or his overtures of support are invitations to enter into a romantic relationship. This may lead to misplaced affections toward the person who provides support and "rescues" us and may, unfortunately, lead to a dramatic relationship. This happens because we don't take the time to fully address our motives so that we can be sure that what we're feeling toward the other person and what he is feeling toward us is real and not based on the emotions of our circumstances. While someone may offer a helping hand or make themselves available to address some of your needs, check your motivation for engaging in this relationship. You just might be prolonging your path to health, well-being, and a drama-free zone. However, if you take the overtures of support at face value and hold off on plunging headlong into a po-tentially dramatic relationship, you will be able to think clearly enough to resolve your most immediate issues and concerns. Doing so gives you the wherewithal to focus on the needs in the next step in your journey toward the drama-free zone: *self-protection.*

In chapter 5, we learned that well-being is contingent on the extent to which we release the negative energy that prevents us from having hope in an optimistic future. At this step toward the drama-free zone, our behavior is motivated by the need for *self-protection*. Having our most fundamental needs met, we aspire to be upwardly mobile and to do whatever it takes to keep us from regressing. In this space, the re-lationships established are safe and often do not require divulging or giving away too much of ourselves. We take few, if any, risks and erect walls to guard our heart and to protect our emotions. And the friend-ships and relationships at this level remain largely superficial. You talk about safe, generic topics with people at the office and socially you have difficulty letting anyone get too close. Your rationale: "I'm just a private person—I don't mix business with pleasure." You have lots of acquaintances but no real friends. Love relationships seem to stall, and it seems like you can never find someone with whom you really have a deep, intimate connection. Have you ever met someone with whom you enjoy working and interacting but never seem to get very close? And then you realize that despite the time spent together, you really don't know them at all. To resolve these needs for self-protection, you'll have to move out from behind the walls you've erected and bravely step out to reveal yourself. This doesn't mean that you remove the walls all at once. Rather, focus on slowly dismantling that wall—one brick at a time. It can be done. Begin by anchoring yourself in your faith so that you have solid footing on which to move out and explore. Then find one person with whom you can share some of your intimate thoughts and feelings. Keep a journal of thoughts and feelings you need to talk about but are not ready to share just yet.

Romance is sometimes born out of a need for self-protection and not so much for love. Women sometimes look for a man who is strong and capable of protecting them and who won't ask for much in return. He may not be the type to require an emotional commitment, but he shares similar interests, and at least initially, seems fun to be with. He also makes most of the decisions in a relationship so that it becomes natural to acquiesce to his suggestions and ideas. Remember Desperanza? She had a need for self-protection in her relationship and unfortunately lost her hopes and dreams in the process. Be careful not to allow your world to revolve around your protector and do not set him up as your savior. Keep the relationship in perspective. Recognize, value, and embrace it for what it is now—a mutually beneficial relationship with someone who shares your interests and ideas. Think twice about plunging headlong into intimacy before you've had a chance to really know who you are, now that you're removing your wall. In the process, you risk losing yourself under the shadow of your partner's persona and strength. You'll substitute this relationship for the wall that once guarded your heart and make yourself vulnerable to a dramatic breakup. True safety and security come when you are willing to take risks and recognize that with them come mistakes, disappointments, and sometimes hurts. But at the same time, these are experiences that can help you learn and grow, build character, and move toward living in the drama-free zone.

As our needs for self-protection are met, we have a keen awareness of our desire for *belonging, social affiliation, love, and acceptance.* Everyone wants to belong and have someone to identify with. In fact, we are hardwired to desire affiliations and to pursue relationships that have meaning for us. Finding new friendships, and rekindling relationships with family members and others who might help engender a sense of connection to the world around us, brings us closer to meeting this need. Doing so provides a network of support when we have seemingly insurmountable challenges in life, including those associated with PDRS. At this point, though, be careful that the romantic relationships you enter into are genuine and based on common goals, values, and interests, not on status seeking or a superficial need for acceptance. Good relationship decision making is the key to resolving this need. You must be thoughtful and honest about why you seek out and engage in particular relationships. Doing so leads to real possibilities for finding love born out of true friendship—the kind we talked about in chapter 4. Keeping your needs in proper perspective and allowing these to grow out of a healthy place and not out of an unmet need for belonging, social acceptance and desirability will enable you to continue charting a path toward living drama-free.

We all want to be viewed in a positive light and thought of favorably. But this can only happen when we esteem ourselves highly and address *unresolved self-esteem needs.* If you value yourself and believe that you have worth, then you can be fully present in your love relationship. Throughout our lives, we receive many messages and engage in numerous interactions that challenge the way we think about ourselves and shape the way we interact with others. Images on television can suggest we are too heavy, too small, too old, or too dark. If we take these messages to heart, we run the risk of seeking approval from others and changing who we are, what we say, and how we think in order to please others. This is why it is so important to draw upon what you've learned about yourself and to have a trusted circle of friends to help you guard against threats to your sense of self. To move forward, you will have to actively and intentionally revisit the relationships you've established and assess whether they are fostering a stronger sense of self or promoting dependence on external opinions. That's not to say that friends who challenge your opinion or hold you to a high standard are not helpful. In fact, the opposite is true. Friends who dare to tell you the truth are the ones you will ultimately appreciate and cherish. It's likely that they too have mastered their own struggles with esteem needs and can now help you find a way forward. Similarly, love at this level must also be uplifting, yet truthful. Having a partner who tells you the truth, even at the risk of putting romance in jeopardy, is rare and precious. So while you might feel some discomfort, embrace it. In the long run, it's what will keep your relationship drama-free and help you to see how truth and love go hand in hand.

Resolving these needs can help you experience life and love in a drama-free zone. In doing so, you develop a strong and healthy sense of self, and your forays into a relationship are not motivated by what others might think or a desire for approval. What should matter and motivate is a deep sense of personal satisfaction at the different ports of call where your relationship journey has taken you. You are attuned to the needs of others and the world around you. You find creative ways to solve problems and continually strive to reach the heights of your potential. In friendship, you are surrounded by like-minded people who care about you enough to tell you the truth and who seek from you the same. In love, you give and you receive. You have done the hard work to establish sufficient trust in your love relationship, to maintain a balance of power, and to achieve the promise of a mutually satisfying partnership.

To be clear, life in the drama-free zone is not a utopia. It has its share of risks and rewards. The key to success in this zone is self-reflection and renewal. Periodically re-examine your needs and determine whether you have difficulty resolving a particular need or whether you're confident to move forward with your relationship. Most importantly, experience what it feels like to live in your drama-free zone so that you'll be less likely to participate in a relationship that might result in PDRS. Express gratitude daily for personal growth and development, and share with others what you have learned and experienced so that you can build a broader network of friends and family who have found a drama-free zone of their own.

Action Plan

What are your strongest needs and why?

What can you do to satisfy these needs?

Identify objectives for meeting these needs.

Identify action steps that will help you accomplish your objectives

1.

2.

3.

4.

CHAPTER 11

Whatever Happened to Jillian?

JILLIAN TOOK MY advice and gave herself the PDRS checkup. She realized that her anger regarding the dramatic breakup with Jason was unresolved and she had been suffering from PDRS. A major sign for Jillian was her incessant need to stay busy enough to avoid ever thinking about her lost love. Jillian finally acknowledged that her dissolved relationship left her deeply wounded and alienated from her friends. Her recovery included making daily lists of things she was grateful for and posting positive affirmations on her bathroom mirror so she could start her day with optimism. This was really hard for Jillian. The breakup left her reeling and struggling with feelings of low self-image and self-worth. After all, Jason's behavior blindsided Jillian. She never imagined that her relationship with him would end the way it did. It was a challenge, but eventually Jillian was able to convince herself that she is a person worthy of love, respect, and trust. Whenever Jillian was tempted to call Jason or drive by his house, she decided instead to take a walk or do something else positive to redirect her energy. On one occasion when Jillian was out walking, she ran into a former college roommate who was in town on business. They hadn't seen each other in years and decided to go to a nearby coffee shop to catch up on old times. As is often the case when women get together, they find themselves talking about men. Jillian listened intently as her friend chatted about the ups and downs of her relationships and how they really challenged her well-being. Then it was Jillian's turn. Her college friend asked, "Jillian how's your love life? What's been going on with you?" Jillian thought for a moment, took a deep breath, and asked,

"Have you heard of Post-Dramatic Relationship Syndrome? That's what I was suffering from after my relationship with Jason ended. Let me tell you about it..."

"Aren't we a pair?" her friend said after listening to Jillian's story. "Is there such thing as genuine love? Should we even be looking for it?"

"Of course," Jillian said. "Despite what happened to me, I believe in love. I think it is wonderful and one of the most powerful emotions there is. But it is also rare and precious. Sometimes it's a diamond in the rough that needs a trained eye to see its complexity and understand its value and beauty. And at other times, it is easily recognizable and familiar. When love is authentic, you know it—it outshines the synthetic and the manufactured emotions. But however love comes to you, whenever it comes to you, cultivate, cherish, and embrace it for however long it lasts—an hour, a day, or a lifetime."

Notes and Reflections
on Finding Your Drama-Free Zone

_____
_____
_____
_____
_____
_____
_____
_____
_____
_____
_____
_____
_____
_____
_____
_____
_____
_____
_____
_____
_____
_____
_____
_____
_____
_____
_____
_____

References

1   Gehrke, Sarah, "Why We Fall in Love: The Science of Love," *Examined Existence*, http://examinedexistence.com/why-we-fall-in-love-the-science-of-love/.

2   "The Science of Love," *Your Amazing Brain*, http://www.youramazingbrain.org/lovesex/sciencelove.htm.

3   Fisher, Helen, *Why We Love: The Nature and Chemistry of Romantic Love. Macmillan, 2004.*

4   Borreli, Lizette, "The Science of Breaking Up: How Heartbreak Hurts Your Physical and Mental Health," *Medical Daily*, October 6, 2014, http://www.medicaldaily.com/science-breaking-how-heartbreak-hurts-your-physical-and mental-health-306320.

5   Obringer, Lee Ann, "How Love Works," *How Stuff Works*, February 12, 2005, http://people.howstuffworks.com/love.htm.